CHARACTER DEPTH

WRITING CRAFT SERIES

CHARACTER DEPTH

keeping readers riveted with real characters, emotion & deep POV

JORDAN McCOLLUM

DURHAM CREST BOOKS

CHARACTER DEPTH © 2015 Jordan McCollum

First printing, 2015

Published by Durham Crest Books
Pleasant Grove, Utah
Set in Linux Libertine

ISBN 978-1-940096-14-8

PRINTED IN THE UNITED STATES OF AMERICA

For all my friends and family members,
who keep me on my intellectual toes

Contents

CHAPTER 3

CHAPTER 4

CHAPTER 5

CHAPTER 6

INTRODUCTION

All readers have come across a book where the characters just didn't grab them, where the characters felt superficial or forced or self-contradictory. A character readers can't relate to is a fatal mistake for a book. Often, this problem boils down to a lack of depth in the character department.

Character depth will mean something different to every reader and every writer, but ultimately, I believe it boils down to being able to see a character as a real person, with all the experiences and opinions and foibles that make each of us real.

To create the impression of depth and reality that we see in the people around us, we need to create a character who is an integrated whole rather than a conglomeration of characteristics that were convenient for the current scene. First, we as writers must see our character who as a complete person. We must see that all his constituent parts and opinions and motivations are pieces of one whole that makes sense as a complete person.

Our characters must be more than puppets who happen to people our plots. To be real and deep and distinctive to your readers, a character must first be real to you, the writer. We must create characters that are fully developed in our minds to build a character that's well-rounded on the page. This includes her personality and appearance as a basic starting point, as well as her history, opinions, relationships and more.

Once we've created this realistic character, we must show this character effectively on the page. To do this, we have to be judicious in choosing which details of our character's thoughts and experiences to share. Conveying their thoughts effectively through deep point-of-view also helps create a three-dimensional character for the reader.

Character depth isn't something that happens by chance. Neither does it come leap onto the page perfectly in the first draft. For a well-rounded character, character creation is a process that begins before the first word hits the page. The process continues through drafting and is further honed and polished in revision. Even if you already have a completed draft—or nearly-published novel—the techniques and principles of character creation are just as important, relevant and effective

Of course, if you've already begun or finished a draft of your project, you probably already have a handle on who your characters are. However, the sections on character creation can still help you round out a character and make sure his constituent parts make sense together.

About the examples in this book

In this text, we rely heavily upon brief, original examples to illustrate each principle. Without authors' commentary on their character creation, it's impossible to delve into their process. Also, I find that using raw, original examples helps writers to envision the writing techniques described and see how to apply them to their work, raw as it may also be, rather than despairing at the "perfection" a polished, published example might seem to possess. This book is meant to encourage you as a writer and instruct you on how to execute these techniques yourself. Original examples show each step of this process while also making the steps more accessible to writers of any skill level. A full list of the examples used in this book appears in the References section.

Well-rounded characters leap off the page and into readers' minds and hearts. They use deep POV, emotion and backstory effectively. And all that begins in the prewriting phase, with effective character creation.

CHARACTER CREATION

Making well-rounded characters
come to life and leap off the page

Preplanning and flexibility

One of the most vital aspects of creating a completely immersive, realistic experience for the reader is your characters. As we prepare to write a new story, writers must think a lot about the characters. Prewriting is a vital part of character creation.

Of course, planning isn't the only part. Although I usually have a good idea of the plot and events of my story, I have found that getting into the character's head and living through her journey in the story always reveals more to me about the character and who she is and how she came to be that way than anything else.

Both the prewriting prep work and the discoveries in the moment are important to creating our realistic characters. The more I prepare and lay the groundwork, the more refined my vision for the character is from the very beginning, and the less I have to revise when I get a character revelation mid-draft. No matter how much prep work you do, it's good to be open to those epiphanies and inspiration about your character. Often your subconscious is simply putting together the pieces you've already provided—so why not start with more pieces for it to play with?

Like every other aspect of our story, our character is further polished in the revision stage. In this chapter, we'll address all three phases of writing when it comes to creating our characters.

Coherent characters

"Narrative cohesion" is the principle that the various parts and aspects of your story must be "coherent," they must make sense together. You can use all kinds of fantastical elements in a story, but it must have some sort of internal consistency, logic or rules that govern the world, and the pieces of the story must have some logical relation to one another.

Our character must similarly have "cohesion." While real people can be a bundle of contradictions, a fictional character must be more "coherent." If we leave our character development to chance, or cobble together a character out of whatever we want them to do in the moment of the story, it's highly likely that the character's actions will seem inconsistent, and the different aspects of the character will no longer make sense.

We strive for internal consistency not because it's "the hobgoblin of little minds" (Emerson's axiom applies only to "foolish consistency"), but because without it, we run the risk of alienating our readers. The character that operates without some ruling sense of internal logic becomes unpredictable and erratic. This character will soon frustrate readers because his actions don't make sense. Finally, readers will close the book and walk away, possibly never to return to your story.

Creating our character to be an integrated, coherent whole is the remedy to this pitfall. When her personality, preferences, motivations and actions make sense together, we have a character that makes much more sense to our reader. This coherent character is the vital foundation to make your character realistic, conveying that sense of character depth.

Our coherent character must be more than an automaton that exists simply to do our bidding and make the plot happen because we said so. The character has to have a life of her own for any story to truly come to life for the reader—and that starts with how we perceive them as the authors and creators of not only this plot but these realistic people. When we perceive them as a realistic, coherent, integrated, rounded person, that comes through in the way our character appears and acts on the page.

Once we're ready to see our character as a three-dimensional person, we're ready to dig into the three dimensions of character.

Three dimensions of character: physical, social, psychological

Many of us begin to build a character with some basic physical description: we know our heroine is a woman, for example, in her late twenties, etc. I often like to find pictures of an actor or model with the right features or personality to use as a visual reference.

As fundamental (and silly) as this seems, it's actually not a bad place to start. The famed dramatist Lajos Egri recommended starting with the physiological aspect of our character. That's not just so we can fill out a police report in case he goes missing. Our physical bodies have a lot to do with what we pursue in life and who we become, from our habits to our occupations. Our self-image is heavily rooted in our appearance and physical capabilities.

Does your character see himself as strong, capable, good looking, or the opposite? Imagine how that would affect something as simple as how the character carries himself. Someone who has a slight build may perceive himself as weak, either consciously or subconsciously. They might walk stooped, or shrink into the shadows, or simply just regard himself as less capable of tasks that require physical exertion. Or does your character's small frame convey power through his bantam strut?

Our physical appearance and bearing also influence how others see us, leading to Egri's second dimension of character, the sociological. If the first dimension dictates how the character interacts with his physical world, this second dimension shows us how he interacts with the other people in that world. Is he pushy or a pushover? Do others respect his authority or make fun of his short-man syndrome behind his back?

Both the physiological and the sociological aspects influence Egri's third dimension of character, the psychological, which shows us how the character interacts with himself. Does she like herself? Is she acutely aware that people are teasing her behind her back, or is she too self-involved to notice? Is she smart, and is that intelligence or lack thereof part of her self-worth? What's she insecure about or afraid of? This is where we really start digging into her personality, how she thinks, which cycles back to influence how she interacts with others and the physical world.

This might sound a little abstract, but the more I develop these dimensions, the more real my characters become to me right from the beginning. In this model, we start off with not only a physical appearance, but a socio- and psychological profile that form his personality, even his quirks. Making sure that these things are really designed together, stemming from one another, helps to create a character who feels like an integrated whole, not a pile of contradictory clichés cobbled together of whatever was convenient to us in the moment of the story.

Many writers begin with some or all of the plot in mind, before a character begins to take shape. Naturally, some of your character can and probably should be dictated by that plot. I almost always know what my character does for a living very early in the prewriting process—sometimes, it's first thing I know about her. If we begin with something like this that's necessary for the plot, we can reverse engineer to get to know him better. If I know my hero is an FBI agent, I need to work within parameters of what kind of person works for the FBI, why he chose that job, and the like. Then I can build from there to backfit the rest of his profile and personality.

As we mentioned, this personality will be revealed and refined even more as we see our character in action in our drafting, interacting with those around him, flaunting those physical and psychological traits—not to mention learning and growing in a character arc. But having a good foundation for the character saves us from flailing around for fifty thousand words until we really discover what makes him tick—I've been there and done that, and the revisions are not pretty.

Revisions, however, are vital to all characters. No matter how well we know our character in prewriting and drafting, we'll have to address issues and smooth him out a bit in revisions.

Bringing our character to life using her core motivations

Quirks and opinions

Once we've started with our character's personality, we can start to make him a unique individual by giving him opinions and preferences. "Giving" is probably the wrong word—just like with our physical attributes and social behavior and psychological profile, we don't want to just throw together whatever's convenient for our story. We want to design a character who feels like a real person, whose personality and physical appearance and preferences all make sense together.

How do we take those dimensions Egri outlined for us and discover these opinions? We have to keep digging. Start with what we know about the character. As I mentioned, I usually know his profession. We might have stumbled across some other interests or hobbies in our character profile so far. If not, take what you know about his personality and think about what he would enjoy in his off hours. Everybody has to do something, right? Does she knit or camp or sing? Does he run or do woodworking or cook? What fits best with what you already know about him?

Note that again, the plot can be a extremely influential here. If we need him to show up at an ad agency or a baseball game or an upscale supermarket, we can again "reverse engineer" that into his character to make the plot and the character work better, and work better together. So maybe he's a small- or medium business owner, a baseball fan, or an amateur chef.

Now we ask questions to dig even deeper on these characteristics. What kind of person enjoys this or chooses this? What does he like about this job? What drew him to it? Is she a spy because it looked cool in the movies? Does he like baseball games for the drama on the field or the food in the stands? How does she keep her apartment? Neat or not? Decorated or plain? What kind of furnishings? What's on her nightstand? What would he order at a restaurant—and what restaurant would he choose in the first place?

No matter what we learn here, we can continue to dig deeper to try to find that core motivation, asking ourselves why he acts in specific ways or what kind of person would live his life.

As you can see, this is a cycle of sorts, so it's possible to start at almost any point and work from there. Start with whatever you know about your character and dig deeper to discover motivations, beliefs and preferences.

The most important discoveries we need to make here are the ones that directly relate to the plot or the character's development. If we're writing a story about a woman overcoming her fears in life—including but probably not limited to a fear of dogs, for example—in order to succeed or be in a relationship, then let's develop this fear of dogs and make sure we show it. This could easily become an incident to show not only her fear of dogs but illustrate her greater fears in life, setting her up for a character arc of growing past her fears.

On the other hand, if we're writing a story about the same character as a high-powered executive who never sees dogs and isn't on an emotional journey to overcome her fears, the fear of dogs could feel forced or tacked on. When we include a character quirk or attitude, our readers will immediately attach significance to that mention. If that characteristic never comes into play for the character or the plot, it seems extraneous—or worse, like a red herring that throws your readers off the real story.

Not everything we discover about our characters has to go into our story, so don't try to force completely unrelated things into the story just to show off how real the character is. Instead, this undermines how real our character seems by making them into a contradictory caricature.

During the drafting process, again, we'll come across points throughout our story where our character might need or express opinions and preferences throughout our story. He prefers ground beef to ground turkey, she believes bonds are the best investment strategy, etc. These incidental opinions will come to us more easily and feel more natural if we know our character better to start off with. Then when we put her into a new situation, it's easier for us to determine how she'll describe and respond to what they encounter because we'll understand what motivates them on a deep level.

As we turn to revision, we must question ourselves about whether the little opinions and thoughts running through our character's minds are significant enough for the story. Here, we must work hard to eliminate anything extraneous and distracting to the reader.

The preferences that don't make it into the story, however, can still be useful, especially as we dig into deep POV. After all, these opinions and preferences are what make your character into an individual, not just a profile.

Relationships

No man is an island, says John Donne. Your character is no different. To be realistic, he needs to have relationships with other people—even if he just landed on an alien planet with amnesia. We've already touched on the sociological dimension of his character, but now we're looking at individual interactions instead of aggregate responses to and from society as a whole.

Normally, you'll have more to work with than an amnesiac astronaut would—friends, family, coworkers. Each of these relationships—including relationships he's not in anymore—has helped to make him the person that he is now. He has a history with all of these people. He and his best friend from high school still joke about that one prank sometimes. His mom will never get over that time he nearly split his sister's head open (even if it really wasn't that close!). He'll laugh with his coworkers about the latest in the series of ridiculous memos from their boss whose hair has really begun to look suspiciously pointy lately.

But relationships aren't just about sharing a past. In fiction, relationships help us to really show how our character acts and thinks. How does she feel about the people around her? Her mom is well-meaning but slightly exasperating, her best friend is hilarious but immature, her one coworker seems to get everything done without breaking a sweat. How does she act toward them? How do they feel and act toward her?

9

The reader's impressions of the character will be more influenced by his actions than by any description, so we need to make sure his actions, and especially interactions with those he's closest to—fit with the psychological and sociological profile we've already worked so hard on. A reader isn't going to buy someone who's supposed to be really kindhearted if all we ever see is him flying off the handle and yelling at people who are just trying to help (unless we really engineer that situation). Remember the personality and profile we've already come up with, both in how those relationships helped to influence how he turned out, and in how his psychology and sociology manifest in that relationship. What kind of mother or best friend or officemate/employee would that person have? How would he feel about and interact with them?

If you have a lot of characters or complex relationships, a relationship map might be helpful. You can keep the connections between the character simple, such as arrows pointing out who loves whom, or you might go into greater detail about how they regard one another.

A blank relationship map and an example are available on my website at http://JordanMcCollum.com/character-depth/

Creating complexity

The first skill we acquire in art class is the ability to draw flat objects. It's not long before we realize that our drawings don't resemble the things we're drawing, and not just because of or lack of skill. To look realistic, our drawings need more than color; they need shading and shadows.

Like the most basic still lifes, our three-dimensional characters need shading and shadows to seem real. Remember as we create our real characters that they're not real people. They're realistic. Fictional people are held to a much higher standard of believability than their real-life, extremely inconsistent counterparts. The truth is stranger than fiction, after all, because fiction has to be believable, while reality is true whether or not we can believe it.

Consistently inconsistent.

In *Poetics*, Aristotle counseled that characters should be good, have appropriate qualities and characteristics (e.g., for his age, gender and station in life), be realistic and be consistent. Aristotle isn't arguing that our character always has to have vanilla ice cream for dessert—he's saying that our characters need to behave in a way that makes sense for who they are. Even if our character's defining trait is that he's inconsistent, then, Aristotle says, he must be "consistently inconsistent."

I'm misappropriating this phrase to expand the meaning. Real people, again, aren't terribly consistent. Our characters don't have to be perfectly consistent or constantly unchanging, either, but the ways in which they're inconsistent should be the same. Without this internal consistency, it's very hard for readers to root for a character that doesn't make any sense— we've all been that reader and it's no fun.

On the other hand, a character who always acts exactly as the reader expects can become boring. The occasional surprise, especially one we've foreshadowed lightly, can sometimes be the final ingredient necessary to make a character really come to life. Surprises like these can take the form of anything from a

11

well-timed joke to an unknown past event to a nuanced and complex, even self-contradictory, emotional response.

Subtlety

This isn't to say that our characters must be completely straightforward and simplistic. Real (and realistic) characters must be as complex and subtle as a real person. We don't need to dump her life history on a complete stranger—the reader. As we touched on in the relationship section, we have to reveal character most of all through his thoughts and actions, not telling the reader what to think about him.

Readers get to know a character the same way they get to know everyone else in their lives—by observing and interacting with them. Most people become proficient at reading others and making inferences about their personality, character and thoughts. As authors, we don't have to hit our readers over the head with information about the character. Some will be slipped in at natural places, and much of it will be filled in through the readers' observations.

Can you make a character too complex or subtle? Of course! If more than one reader comes back with questions about a particular action or aspect of a character, there's a good chance we've gone too far here. Also, we have to make sure to take the time to get our readers emotionally invested in our characters— and not by pointlessly withholding information about them to build false mystery—before we throw too many clues about the character's secrets at them. If readers don't care about the character, they definitely won't care about the clues!

Perhaps most important in this concept is to remember that our characters must be more than just the people who happen to do the things in our stories, the puppets who people our plots. While not everything we brainstorm will come into play in our pages, the more we see our characters as these real people with attitudes and preferences and emotions, the more we can convey them as real people on the page. A lack of character depth often stems from a writer seeing his or her character as little more than the means to the end—the way that we can execute our plot.

This real, coherent character is also a product of her life experiences, including those that took place before our story begins. Backstory can be an excellent way to deepen our characterization—when it's handled effectively.

2

HISTORY LEADING TO GROWTH: BACKSTORY

A well-rounded character must give readers
the sense that he existed before the story

A well-rounded character must give readers the sense that he existed before the story began (and will continue to exist once they finish the story). In addition to the appearance, quirks, opinions and relationships we discussed in the previous chapter, our character must have backstory in order to seem real.

Backstory refers to all the events of the character's life that happen before the present of the story. It's helpful to a writer to know quite a bit about your character's life before the story, including those attitudes and relationships we've mentioned already. We'll probably also know about several major events in our character's life before the story began.

However, we can't—and shouldn't—try to wedge his every memory into the present story. Only the most pertinent and vital experiences should make it onto the page. They must help to drive the plot or the character's emotional growth, or they are more likely to detract and distract than develop depth.

What to include and what to leave out

As with our character's quirks or attitudes, when we include a piece of backstory, our readers will immediately attach significance to that mention. And just as with quirks and attitudes, if that experience never comes into play for the character or the plot, it seems extraneous—or worse, like a red herring that throws your readers off the real plot. It serves only to distract your readers as they try to decipher why you attached such significance to a past event, when in reality that event is *not* significant or even relevant to the story.

The litmus test for what backstory to leave out and what backstory to include is deceptively simple. Does this event propel the plot forward or influence character growth in some way? Does it illustrate something vital about the character or the present story's events to give it greater meaning? If the answer to either of these questions is yes, we can include this past experience with confidence.

Once we've determined that a piece of backstory is worth including, we need to figure out *when* to use that event in the context of the present story. Two major methods of backstory timing are both excellent. The first is to convey backstory early on, setting up a major revelation or change. This method builds anticipation as your readers are clued into a past event and are searching for the significance, trying to understand why we've included it.

The second method is to wait until that backstory plays into the present story: shortly before or after a pivotal moment in the present story. This is especially effective when the event imbues an already powerful moment with even greater significance or meaning.

The last thing we must determine about a vital piece of backstory is *how* to convey it. Be careful about the narrative mode you select to convey the backstory. Most of the available modes are more fraught with perils than ancient Greek dramas. A flashback can show a well-developed scene, but it brings the narrative of the present story—and its tension—to a jarring halt. Summarizing the backstory in narration or dialogue can bog readers down in boring information dumps.

Generally, effective backstory is conveyed as efficiently as possible and as appropriate to its significance. The protagonist's memory of his late wife as he searches for her killer is highly significant and charged with emotion, so it warrants a fuller development. His memory of their routine trip to an ice cream parlor, however, can probably be effectively conveyed in a sentence or two, if at all.

Tension is another key consideration in incorporating backstory. Because it can pause or slow down the present story, backstory can be lethal to tension. We must pay careful attention to what's happening in the present story as we try to convey this backstory to avoid undercutting tension or dumping information on our readers. We can use conflict to convey backstory—having our characters argue about a past event rather than one monologuing about it. We can also use background tension as we present information such as backstory.

Pseudonymous screenwriting blogger Mystery Man on Film cites a classic example of this in *Raiders of the Lost Arc.* As they convey technical details and backstory about the medallion and the height of the staff, the viewers could easily get bored. The filmmakers kept the viewers' interest by keeping the tension high as the little monkey snatches dates from the characters' plate—and dies. Oblivious, our hero Indiana Jones nearly eats the dates several times throughout the scene, keeping the viewers glued to the present story while they convey this important backstory.

Perhaps the most important kind of backstory is the one that sets up the character's journey of emotional growth: her character arc.

Character arcs: backstory leading to growth

You can have the greatest plot in the world but if your character is flat your book will be, too. For a character to truly resonate with readers, she should change and grow over the course of the story. For more powerful characters, focus not just on the external plot, but the characters' internal journey as well.

Every character, and every character arc, has to start somewhere. If you're familiar with the hero's journey, you know that in the ordinary world, something is amiss—something is missing from the protagonist's life. That doesn't just mean a love interest or a murderer that needs to be brought to justice—there's something deeper, on an emotional level, that the character needs, something he lacks. This need often stems from a specific event or pattern of events in the character's past: his backstory.

As taught in Jami Gold's excellent blog series, screenwriter Michael Hauge has a great model for using backstory in a character journey. We start with the character's unfulfilled, a need, a void. The character has what Hauge calls a "wound" in their backstory, this specific traumatic event or pattern of traumatic events. This wound causes the character to form a mistaken belief about himself or the world, often due to fear. The event may force the character to change how he sees the world or himself, or it may prompt her to act in a way not true to herself, changing who she is to avoid that same situation again.

Either way, the wound leads the character to assume a "mask"—the lie he tells himself, way he present himself to the world. Throughout the character's emotional journey, he'll be fighting his ingrained belief about himself to reach his true "essence," who he really is or wants to be despite that belief.

To make this a little more concrete, Hauge uses the example of *Shrek*. Shrek's wound is that people have always run from him. So he believes he must be terrifying and no one would want to be around him. He's afraid of rejection, so he rejects others first. He assumes a mask of a scary ogre to protect himself from going through that kind of rejection again. But his true essence is someone who does want those connections—friends, love.

Another good example of this would be the movie *Frozen*. From her perspective, Anna spent her childhood rejected by her older sister and erstwhile best friend, Elsa. Elsa refused to even open the door to see her sister for years. Anna formed a mistaken belief that her sister didn't want to see her.

A note about backstory execution

The filmmakers chose to show the backstory, or the background information to the story, at the beginning of *Frozen*. When Elsa's cryokenetic powers are revealed and she secludes herself in an ice palace, Anna endeavors to reason with her sister. But as she arrives at the palace doors, she hesitates. We've seen her fruitlessly knocking at her sister's door for over a decade. Now, facing those doors between them again, Anna's afraid of being rejected again. This powerful storytelling takes no words on Anna's part (she only notes after the doors open, "That's a first"), but her wound is obvious.

Usually the most convenient way to show the initial starting place of a character arc is through an event where the character acts from the mistaken belief and it backfires, hurting him somehow. Even if he doesn't realize how much that mask is crippling him, the readers will see that it's holding him back from what he truly wants in life.

This event, early on in the story, is often a catalyst for the external plot as well. The external events of the story, in turn, directly influence the character's emotional journey. A well-executed internal character journey is intertwined with the external plot. Not only do the events of the plot show the character's starting and ending points, but the external plot events also force the change, and show the stages of the journey throughout the story. The backstory may not ever be specifically shown or stated—Shrek doesn't have a flashback to one particular rejection—but its cumulative effects will be felt throughout the book through the character's emotional journey of growth.

For more information on character arcs and how to effectively execute them, see my book *Character Arcs: Founding, forming and finishing your character's internal journey.*

Discovering & engineering your character's backstory for maximum impact

As writers, we need to remember that we are the architects of not only our plots, but our character as well. This means we can—and must—engineer his past for the best effect. We're not talking about tacking on some tragic backstory so the reader pities our character and excuses his reprehensible actions—that doesn't work. Instead, we must look at the journey we've given our character and figure out why she is the way she is at the beginning. How did she form this mistaken belief? What would make someone view herself or the world that way? Most importantly, how can we relate it to the action of our story?

This vital backstory should be:

- **Related to the present story**. We might accomplish this using Hauge's model by making it the character's wound, or we might tie it into the external plot, directly grappling with those wounds as the main story progresses.
- **Surprising but alluded to**. Well-balanced foreshadowing through our character's attitudes and actions can help create this sense.
- **Revealed at the most impactful time**. Again, this may be early on to create a sense of anticipation, or it may come at the time when the emotional significance of the event plays into the story directly.
- **Resolved at the climax** through the character's growth in the story and their final choices to reverse their behavior in the ultimate moment of character change, as she faces down and finally overcomes the antagonist.

As with our character himself, we want his past to be an integrated part of both him and the story. We need to dig beyond picking some random traumatic event and look at his journey in the process of the story.

If he's learning to face fears, we need to give him a legitimate experience to create those fears. While we don't want to make that experience a straight repeat of our current plot or its climax, the two experiences will necessarily have some similarities and parallels. The major difference of course will be in the character's reaction because of her experiences of growth in the course of our novel.

What kind of experience do we need? That depends heavily upon the character and his journey—and the situations the plot will put him in. Those external situations prompt the internal growth, so we need to find ways to force the character to make real choices (not just whatever any decent human being would do) toward or away from their post-arc state, their essence in Hauge's model.

To find this experience, once again, we'll start with what we know and dig deeper. Let's say we know our character has a strength of bravery. She knows how to face fear and act. We can convert this into a weakness or a wound by digging deeper into the Why? behind her bravery. Why is she so brave? What in her history made her brave? Was she the oldest of abandoned siblings, so she had to put on a courageous front? Did she survive cancer, and now believes nothing else could be nearly that bad? Was her best friend victimized, and she'll never let that happen to someone else?

Once we've brainstormed our ideas on the character's past, we can select which of these suits the current story's plot best without being repetitive. We might need to keep digging to weigh our options, examining what would have the greatest emotional impact and resonance (on the character and the readers) in light of our plot or arc.

As we brainstorm reasons behind a character trait, we can often discover how it's either a weakness or hiding a weakness as well. If she's brave because an adult role was foisted upon her at a young age, perhaps she has a tendency to take that responsibility to a level of self-blame or recrimination—or maybe she can't tolerate people who don't show responsibility. If she's a survivor, she might lack empathy for people who struggle with smaller crises or who lose hope. If she's protecting her best friend (retroactively & by proxy), she could be overprotective, closed off to others, or too mistrustful.

The events or circumstances of her backstory led to her forming a mistaken belief that guides her life now. Healing these wounds, correcting these beliefs, allows her to become the person she truly should be to ultimately prevail over the antagonist in the climax of the story. And now we're ready to execute this character arc.

The techniques of character creation and arcs are only the beginning of conveying character depth. We must also show our character by using deep POV to depict their thoughts and keep our readers engaged with well-executed emotions.

DEEP POINT-OF-VIEW

Deep POV conveys your character most effectively. Seeing all her reactions and thoughts, presented exactly as she perceives them, gives readers the greatest possible insight into a well-rounded character.

Deep POV is the most popular narrative mode used in fiction today. It's a vital key to a truly immersive experience in fiction—when it's done right!

Simply put, deep point-of-view or deep POV is narrating from inside your character's head, whether you're in first or third person. Other narrative modes include an omniscient POV that can see into everyone's thoughts, an external narrator who can see into no one's, or a limited POV, where you occasionally dip into the thoughts of one character at a time.

Deep POV is different because you're not just sharing the occasional thought or reaction from one or more characters. You're telling the story as if the character himself were telling it, using his phrases or her vocabulary. Perhaps the ultimate deep POV is to channel everything through the character's voice instead of the author's. Everything the readers get is as if they were seeing it through that character's eyes and mind. They don't just watch this character and his actions—they don't look at the character looking out the window. They see what he sees through the window. They seem to live the character's experiences themselves.

Deep POV is key to character depth because it helps to convey your character most effectively. Seeing all her reactions and thoughts, presented exactly as she perceives them, gives readers the greatest possible insight into a well-rounded character.

Getting to know your character from the inside out

To effectively execute our deep POV, we must know what the

world looks like from inside our character's minds. The prewriting groundwork that we've done in discovering our character's personality, relationships and preferences is a great place to start. But how do we convey that on the page?

While I'm not a fan of drawn-out character questionnaires with a plethora or immaterial questions, I do find it much easier to write if I have a good understanding of the characters—and writing a character journal helps to firm up my ideas and give me concrete sense of who the character is and how he thinks. (Many people advocate and enjoy extensive character questionnaires to get to know their character in minute detail. If that's worked for you in the past, I recommend continuing it.)

For me, my favorite way to get to know a character is to write something short from that character's first-person viewpoint, especially if that character doesn't use a first-person viewpoint in the story. Sometimes I'll pick a specific point in the story to "set" this character journal, usually either right before or right after the beginning. Even if I neglect this prewriting step until my writing process is well underway, I make discoveries about the character's motivations and actions, who he is and why he acted the way he did.

One of the most important steps of any exercise to get acquainted with your characters is to *act* as you write: really pretend to be that person, experiencing these feelings, thoughts and events. How do you feel about what has happened?

You might also try rewriting scenes from your story in first person. As you write, again, act, pretend. Close your eyes and visualize what happens in the scene, but not as someone else might see it—from the character's vantage point. What do you notice? How does that make you feel? What do you think about?

First person, third person & italics

Both first and third person can be done in deep POV. (Sometimes it's hard *not* to do deep POV in first person!) What makes a point of view "deep" is how "close" we are to the viewpoint character's thoughts. In a distant third-person mode, the reader may be privy to a few of the character's direct thoughts, and those are always related in italics. His actions and speech are vital to characterize and help readers understand him. Often, the reader is acutely aware of what the viewpoint character's doing, as if watching him with a tight focus, and every once in a while there's a voiceover of his thoughts.

In deep POV, the character's thoughts can form almost a running commentary on the actions of the story. We don't just get the occasional *The problem with blackmail is that it's like a gun with only one bullet* (*Burn Notice*) or *Yeah, the mob isn't exactly known for its cushy retirement and severance package* (*Saints & Spies*). Statements like that—direct thoughts from the viewpoint character's mind—are woven into the narration. In very deep POV, those statements do not need to be italicized because then everything would be italicized! You might still italicize a thought if the character shifts from third to first person (or vice versa) or from past tense narration of the story to present tense reaction. For example, contrast:

> Michael settled into his chair. Unbelievable. Was this going to take all day?
>
> versus
>
> Michael settled into his chair. *I can't believe this! Is this going to take all day?*

The first example is entirely in past tense and third person, but we're still getting his thoughts pretty much verbatim. Both might be considered deep POV, but in my opinion, the first is a deeper narration mode because the narration itself comes directly from his thoughts instead of using a red flag, italics, to announce to the reader, "WE WILL NOW HEAR A WORD FROM MICHAEL ON THIS ISSUE!" (There are also divergent opinions on whether the "unbelievable" would be italicized in the first example; I tend toward saying no, especially with the unitalicized follow-up thought right after it.)

First person is the same way. As long as we remember to include the character's observations and thoughts and reactions—in her voice—rather than just reporting on those actions, we should be able to maintain that deep POV. In fact, in a book where the character has a very strong voice and a lot of thoughts and opinions to share, first person can be the most liberating and most fun—and by some measures, the best voice for the story and the character. A less strong voice, however, may be better handled in third person.

Making your character's voice distinctive

We've already done some exercises to get to know our character better, to dig into what makes her unique, what she likes, how she feels. Now we're going to take all that information and use it to make our character's voice distinctive.

What they notice

Your character's personal interests will deeply influence the things that stand out to him in his environment. Our personal interests often filter what we see around us. Similarly, character's personal interests, hobbies and profession not only filter what he notices, but his diction, the words he uses to describe it—from the scenery to the events to the other people in the story.

Does your character have a passion for painting? Collect baseball cards and rare comics? Live for the dance? Everyone has something he loves—hobbies, interests, even his occupation. All of these things can easily influence what someone notices and how he talks about it.

To use an example, let's say our characters are a family visiting a museum:

- An architect might admire the layout of the museum or the aesthetics of the building's design and exterior.
- Her dabbling-in-interior-decorating sister is more focused on the color scheme, the flow of traffic through the museum and the arrangement of displays.
- Their hobby-Egyptologist mother wants to hurry up and get to the mummies.
- Their wannabe-artist father, of course, is there for the art. He's the only one who really notices the paintings (but he barely glances at the desiccated bodies).

The characters' personal interests and hobbies dictate what they notice most, what they spend the most time looking at, what they analyze. They'll easily gloss over things that don't fall into their special categories of interest.

Our character will also use the specific vocabulary of his passion—his interests or hobbies or profession—to describe those things that he notices. A cop will describe a room or a person differently from his executive fiancée, and they'll both see things differently from their wedding planner.

The police officer might notice exits, vantage points, or safe positions. The businesswoman focuses on the costs of the venue, whether its branding is "on point" (in general or for their wedding) or making a deal with the owners. The wedding planner's envisioning the space, planning decorations and trying to sell her clients on her vision.

With a person, the police officer will quickly size up her trustworthiness. He might define her as the "criminal type" or analyze her body language. The executive may home in on whether this is someone she can work with or negotiate with or manage. The wedding planner is just trying to make everyone happy!

We may not be law enforcement officers or Egyptologists ourselves, but when we know that kind of detail about our character, with a little research and thought, we can use that information to deepen her characterization and her voice.

This may seem like it's excessively narrowing our voice,

putting blinders on our character. However, a character doesn't have to completely ignore something significant simply because it doesn't fall into her "interests" box. Rather than narrowing our character's world and voice, we're refining it, developing her as a real person as well by making her voice distinctive.

I, for example, can't tell a sloop from a schooner. But someone who spends every weekend on his sailboat is going to have a full vocabulary for not just every type of ship, but the masts, the rigging, the knots and everything else. If this is how he fundamentally defines himself, he'll often use "nautical" terms—the vocabulary of his passion.

When he meets a beautiful woman, he won't describe her in fashion terms. Instead, he'll use his own natural vocabulary. He might describe how she moves through the crowd like a cutter slicing through the waves. She could have eyes the color of the sea or hair the same shade as the burnished mahogany fittings of his cabin.

The more parallels our character can draw to the things around him and his passions, the more likely he is to notice those things and like those things.

The character's attitude toward the things and people around him is another important aspect of his character—and his voice. Perhaps most importantly, character attitudes are a strong characterization tool. When readers see how someone feels about the world around him, they really get to know him. If he recoils at a church and quotes Karl Marx ("Religion . . . is the opiate of the masses."), readers know him more deeply than if the author just stated, "Jimmy hated religion."

Again, his interests, hobbies and profession can influence this heavily. Our sailor friend might consider a man whose only maritime experience was on a ferry to be a troglodyte. Let's say our sailor is stuck in an urban environment. Freeway tunnels are the epitome of all that's wrong with the city—they're closed in, suffocating, dark, crowded, and most of all, nothing like the freedom of sailing, the open ocean, the wind in your face.

On the other hand, he loves taking his lunch on the observation deck of his office building—when the wind is right, you get a breeze from the sea. He has an immediate affinity for people who strike him as sailors. And your Nautica bathroom decor? Well, you decide—he could either love the touch of sailing in your home, or he could think you're a total poseur.

A slob might not even see the pile of clean socks on the floor (or are they dirty?), simply walking past. But her neat-freak roommate is sure to notice—and she sees whether they're clean, dirty, or a mix of the two—and then what does she think of her slovenly roommate? If the neat-freak is a housekeeper or professional organizer, does she have a specific term for someone like her roomie?

All of these techniques help us key into the unique voice of our character, presenting a voice that's just as integrated and coherent as our character herself.

Deep POV mechanics

In addition to using our character's phrases and interests to dictate what they notice and how they talk about it, there are a number of writing mechanics that can make our deep POV even smoother. This doesn't entail changing your voice or prescribing the one and only way anyone can ever do deep POV; these are simply keys to making your deep POV as smooth and effective as possible.

While there are many more techniques of deep point-of-view, truly showing and using detail are the two that most effectively help to convey a real sense of the character and portray them as a well-rounded person.

Show, don't tell—for real

The deeper the POV, the more important it is to show instead of tell. In a fairly limited POV, you often get only the character's conclusions: "This lady's dowdy." "That guy was tall." In the real world, our minds notice details and then we put those specific details to come to a conclusion. When we structure our fiction the same way, our readers can better follow the character's logic. So presenting more of the character's thought process not only makes more sense and shows his voice and unique take on the world more, but it's also deeper POV.

Contrast these two:

Annie turned around to find a very tall, very angry man looming behind her.

versus

Annie turned around to find a set of shirt buttons. Shirt buttons? She followed the column of buttons up, her neck arching back to peer at the scowl looming above the crisp collar.

In both passages, we get that the man's considerably taller than Annie, and that's he unhappy. You could take the showing further by describing the scowl. This all depends on the context and its pacing—if she's only got enough time to catch a glimpse of him before he robs her or hits her or runs away, you'll want to skip to the conclusion. If meeting this man is important or you want a specific effect, you can draw it out even more.

This showing requires you to create images that your readers can visualize through specific detail.

Use detail

Detail helps to sets readers in the story's milieu. Using our character's interests and passions as a guide to what she notices and how she talks about it, we can convey a stronger sense of the events, people and places in our story.

Be specific in your details. Specific images convey much more meaning than vague, generic references. A Beemer gives a very different interpretation than a beater, and both of which are more useful to us as writers than the word "car." Again, these specific details build to a logical conclusion, drawing our readers along with our character's thoughts. The conclusions our characters reach about people, places and events are more powerful when they're supported by details. But instead of laying out the character's conclusion and then backing it up with the specific evidence, we must take things in a logical order to make those conclusions comprehensible and powerful.

Here's another comparison to illustrate the power of showing the details, then telling the conclusion:

Jack hid in the corner just before Erica walked in. She was eager to see him. She scanned the room for him.

This example has no true details and presents a conclusion first. Rather than showing the details and forming a natural conclusion, we're just telling that conclusion.

Let's say Jack works in a job where he needs to be able to interpret people's reactions—law enforcement, perhaps. He would watch and describe her reaction in more detail:

Jack hid in the corner just before Erica walked in. Leaning forward, she cast her eyes about hopefully, eyebrows drawn up as if she silently asked herself where he was. She was eager to see him.

This paints a much more vivid picture. With these details, the readers see what Jack sees. In this instance, the details might be so self-explanatory and its meaning so obvious that we don't need to tell the conclusion at all.

Even showing, however, has its reasonable limits. The amount of detail—or even its use at all—depends on the context of the scene and its pacing. We can skip to conclusions in the middle of a car chase. The hero and heroine meeting for the first time calls for a bit more notice of detail. To keep the character's thoughts "feeling" like they're happening in real time, be sure to match the amount of detail—and how you work it in—with the pacing.

Deep POV is an opportunity to show our character as a real person, to make her personality run deeper than superficial thoughts or only what might be observed from the outside looking in. Often, using deep POV is the key to bringing our character to life for the reader.

Once we've mastered our character's voice, we must get the reader onboard through character sympathy and keep them there with well-written emotion.

EFFECTIVE EMOTION

Character sympathy and effective, well-written emotions immerse your readers in your characters' experiences.

Once we've created our three-dimensional character, we must make sure she remains real to the reader through effectively conveying her emotions. This technique is just as vital as POV to immerse your readers in your characters' experiences. But first, we need to make sure we create reader sympathy with our characters—it's not automatic!—and then we need to present our character's emotions in the most natural and accessible way.

Creating character sympathy

Character sympathy is how we get our reader on board for the character's emotional journey. We get the reader to tune into what the character is feeling so the reader will *care* about what happens to the character. Sometimes we think this is an automatic process for the reader, but the truth is, sympathy isn't automatic; it's earned. Even unlikeable characters can be sympathetic—if we as writers work to create that sympathy.

Strength

The first ingredient in our sympathy formula is strength. All characters must have some strength, some fortitude of character, some inner resource, some poise—something to show the readers why they would want to sympathize with, or look up to, or just flat out be this person.

Outer strengths are typically easy to find by looking at whatever the character is uniquely good at: physical strength, skills, talents, hobbies, profession. But more than that, a character's strength is something indomitable within her. Many character traits count as a character strength, including:

- Perseverance

- Self-control
- Optimism
- Self-sacrifice
- Wit or humor
- Integrity

However, if you don't already know your character's specific inner strengths, discovering them can be more tricky. To find your character's inner strength, we can turn back to his motivations again and what we've learned from creating our character or seeing him in action. What makes him get up in the morning? What is her ultimate goal in life? What does he do when his wife is in danger and all hope of saving her is lost? How does she react when someone comes between her and the man she loves? What does he do (or want to do) when his boss or mother or wife says, "Take a hike"?

The answer will be different for every character—but few readers really want to spend eight or more hours in the head of someone who would answer "nothing" to any one of those questions. While readers do understand someone who struggles, someone with a sad past, someone facing a difficult choice, letting your character just roll over and take it is intensely frustrating to a reader.

Along with strength, struggles are necessary to make sure our character doesn't become too perfect.

Struggle

The second ingredient in our character sympathy formula is struggles. Contrary to popular opinion, the reader does NOT have to pity the character to identify with him, but you have to let the reader see your character struggling. (I doubt I need to clarify this, but just in case: struggling with how incredibly awesome he is doesn't count.)

External struggles are okay here. While we know that the character's past will strongly influence her present, being mired in that terrible past isn't a good way to create character sympathy. We need another kind of struggle, one more directly tied to the present plot. For example, the character might work against an antagonist, whether a person or an impersonal force. The antagonist, especially at the beginning, should actually win. We're cultured to side with the underdog, the Cinderella story, the person who has been wronged. Failure can contribute to sympathy as well as move the plot forward.

The antagonist may be a supervillain, but more likely, the antagonist is simply someone who stands in the way of our hero's goals—it need not even be the ultimate "Big Bad" guy the character will face at the climax. It may even be an opposing force within the character himself through dramatic inner conflict. Thus this struggle may be an epic battle or a smaller, more personal fight.

Internal struggles can make this character even more realistic, more relatable. Several types of struggles "count" for creating character sympathy, including:

- Resisting the call to adventure
- Self-doubt
- Embarrassment
- Being weaker than the antagonist
- Loneliness

- Fear

No matter what struggles our character faces, make sure that the character is invested enough in her goal that she must push forward despite the struggle, even though each setback does affect her personally. If it would make more sense to walk away and that's a viable option, why would reader want to watch or cheer for him to torture himself for no good reason? Instead, we must make sure our character *has* to fight and cannot simply walk away. Each setback on his journey resonates with him on a deep level. The character must care if we want the reader to care, too.

Sacrifice

The third vital ingredient to creating character sympathy is sacrifice, putting someone else's needs or desires before his own, doing something that benefits someone else more than the character himself. This noble goal doesn't have to be doing something for the greater good, making the planet a better place or achieving world peace. Even a small goal that benefits the character's own children shows that he is capable of caring about someone or something else more than he cares about himself. It shows readers that the character has the capacity to see others' needs and problems, and that, for at least this one instance, he can set aside the selfish impulses we all have and think of someone else. Even if it's the only glimpse readers have of the character's potential for growth, it's an important one.

It isn't enough to simply tell readers how your character embodies these three ingredients to sympathy. We must *show* them. Ultimately, reader identification is won and lost through the character's actions. Mystery Man on Film states it well: "It's what we see the character do in the present that determines how much we will or will not care about that character."

Screenwriters focus on this idea heavily, because character action is all they have to develop a character. Screenwriter Blake Snyder believed this element of action to create character sympathy was so important, he named his book of screen-writing principles after it: *Save the Cat!* However, the title is a little misleading. Taken out of context, it sounds like we're being urged to throw in some unrelated heroic act early in the course of the work to make the reader like the character.

That isn't what Snyder advocates. He defines the principle as "The hero has to *do* something when we meet him so that we like him and want him to win" (121, emphasis added).

Note that the actual rule doesn't state the act has to be particularly heroic, or unrelated to the plot, or actually involve felines. It's simply a principle of action, to remind us that a character doesn't win our readers' hearts simply by being cool or capable or flashy, and it's as true in the latest Hollywood blockbuster as in the quietest literary novel.

If we're not careful about our characterization and showing his actions, those actions can begin to look like superfluous add-ons designed to trick readers into liking this guy. Our goal isn't to manipulate readers but to have our character demonstrate to our readers why he deserves to share his story, why he matters. We must make our character's actions that show this organically related to the story and the character.

Inner conflict

Readers don't have as much of a chance to sympathize with someone who immediately does the right thing, especially if he's quickly rewarded for it. Some of the greatest, most compelling characters are those that struggle against some part of them that doesn't want to do what he knows he should—for reasons the reader knows and understands (it's difficult, dangerous, etc.). The struggle of inner conflict is very important to establishing reader sympathy and to creating a character who feels realistic.

Inner conflict allows us to show more facets of our characters, which always helps to make them more well-rounded. But more than that, it brings the events of the plot home to our character and our reader. It shows readers why the character cares about the events of the plot, helping the reader to care, too.

For a full treatment of developing character sympathy, see my book *Character Sympathy: creating characters your readers have to care about.*

Now that we've got our readers on board the emotional roller coaster, let's buckle up and take them on a ride.

Show, don't just tell, with emotions

The major pitfall most of us face when writing emotions is falling into the trap of telling. But to engage our readers, simply stating "she was scared" or "he was angry" isn't going to suffice.

Clichés, automatic turns of phrase like "his blood boiled," aren't helpful either. These phrases are used so often they don't carry much meaning anymore. Even gestures can become cliché. Avoid telling through clichés and work harder to convey realistic and effective emotion—change it up and make it fresh instead of giving your readers something to gloss over.

Stating the emotion or using a stock phrase robs the scene of its power. Psychologists teach parents that they should help their children label their emotions. Giving an emotion a name saps its power over you, and the same holds true in our writing when we tell the emotion instead of showing the character's experience.

We want to do this through both actions and thoughts. Blogger Ray Rhamey has a great example of executing this principle on his blog FloggingTheQuill.com. He takes the before example, "Anna was physically and mentally exhausted," and demonstrates how to really *show* this feeling:

All Anna wanted to do was crawl into bed and go to sleep. But first she would cry. She didn't think she could be calm and composed for another minute.

Here, the example relies on getting deep into the character's thoughts. We should be on this level of deep POV with the character much of the time. That level of access to the character's thoughts and feelings draws the reader in. Showing emotions in deep POV easily circumvents readers' "defenses," making them not only suspend disbelief but drawing them into the story and the character by tapping into the readers' deep-seated emotions.

Using action is another technique to show emotion. To use another FloggingTheQuill.com example:

He stabbed the man furiously.

Here's a good example of one reason we should use adverbs with caution: they're red flags for instances of telling. We're taking all the power out of this emotion by stating it flat-out. Contrast that with Rhamey's fix:

He plunged the dagger into the man's chest again and again and again, screaming "Die!" each time the blade stabbed into flesh.

Notice that this example doesn't name the emotion. Can you tell what it is? Of course! Would using the word "anger" add anything? No, it would be redundant or trite. Instead of relying on just thoughts to get the emotion, the reader truly sees that rage through the character's actions. Setting or props can also be used similarly to show emotion.

Figurative language

Figurative language, such as metaphors and similes, is one of the best ways to show an emotion. The imagery here can be so vivid that you might not need to name the emotion at all.

Contrast these two sentences:

Calla was afraid

> versus
>
> A cold child crept down her back as if on spider's legs.

Which one draws you in? Which one makes you feel the fear?

This figurative language can be even more powerful and draw reader into the story and the characters even more when we work hard to use language specific to our character. If your main character is a veterinarian, perhaps she thinks of fear like an animal backed into a corner, and describes each of her actions and responses that way (arching her back, snarling, barking, etc.).

Or maybe he's a veteran—he sees the world divided along battle lines, can't shake the memories of those he's lost, or is just ready for all this fighting to be over. This is another opportunity to incorporate those preferences and interests and hobbies we've worked so hard on, plus using your deep POV skills again to keep the reader right there, feeling each spidery step on her spine.

Visceral emotion, visceral response

We can take this to an even deeper level with the occasional visceral response.

Obviously, writing "she felt sad" or "he was scared" isn't going to cut it. We want our readers to feel what our characters feel, and characters—people—experience emotion physically.

Emotions engage our bodies. Even emotional clichés attempt to show this: seeing red, blood boiling, butterflies in the stomach.

To get to our readers' emotions, we need to use our character's emotions. As I've said before, we want our readers to experience these emotions right along with our character. Techniques like figurative language, when focused on physical reactions to emotions, almost bypass a reader's conscious thoughts, evoking similar physical responses from the reader. That's why they're so powerful—and why we must use them judiciously.

In Margie Lawson's Empowering Character Emotions course (and her EDITS system), she uses a special classification for an involuntary physical response to an emotional situation—the most powerful type of emotional response. Things like sweating, blushing, skin tingling, and other responses to extreme emotion pack a powerful punch. We have to work hard to keep these responses fresh—we don't want to repeat the same body part or those tired old clichés—and they're most effective if used sparingly.

Figurative language using the character's specific vocabulary and visceral responses are more challenging methods of showing character emotions, and they work best in tandem. But these methods are the most vivid, the most individual, and the best way to illustrate the feelings and the character, showing all her facets. These methods should still used in moderation—especially involuntary physical responses and similes/metaphors. Too many, even if they're all spot-on, can distract the reader, making the emotion feel more external. Instead of a person with emotions, it starts to feel like a collection of body parts and autonomic responses.

Of course, this is all easier said than done. Showing character emotions in a unique and engaging way is a challenge, no matter how many times you've done it before. (In some ways, it gets harder over time, since you continually have to fish for new ideas to avoid repeating yourself.) Don't pressure yourself to get this all right on the first try, or even the first draft. Human emotions are tricky things—and in writing, we should be grateful we get multiple attempts to get them right!

All these methods need to work together to create effective, realistic emotion in a scene—and every scene should have some emotion. In a highly emotional scene, we'll stack several effects, weaving them together for max impact.

Emotional structure & flow

After highly emotional scenes, for me, the next most difficult type of emotion to convey is multiple emotions in a single scene. Although most passions are composed of multiple emotions, we typically don't experience, say, love, ambivalence and annoyance all the same time. But sometimes we need our characters to.

If these emotions are responses to several different stimuli within a scene, it makes sense to have different responses. It's more of a challenge in the emotional aftermath of the action of a scene. However, a simple structure can help with this kind of emotional arc.

In *Scene & Structure*, Jack Bickham gives a structure for the sequel, the emotional response to the action of a scene: Emotion – Thought – Decision – Action (51). The Emotion is the initial response to the events of the scene and its Disaster.

When the character moves past the initial emotion, they think through the events, their response and their options in the Thought phase. This ultimately leads to a Decision, which takes the character to another Action, setting up another scene.

Not all the steps of the sequel are necessary. In fact, the sequel itself might not be necessary—depends on the pacing and whether the emotional reaction constitutes a change. But when the character is going through a major turning point, we can spend a little more time here. And this is where we motivate the next action.

When an emotional change in the sequel follows the full steps of the sequence, the sequel shows a logical progression of events. By moving through these steps, we can lead the character and the readers through the change and create a compelling, convincing transformation. Each phase of the sequence can layer on another aspect of the emotion, creating multifaceted contrast.

For example, if we need our character to go from shocked after the last disaster to furious in the sequel, we start with that initial emotional response—the shock. We don't have to spend a long time exploring the shock, especially if that's a predictable, understandable reaction in light of the scene.

Once we create a vivid picture of the shock (a difficult emotion to portray, since it's characterized by the absence of feeling), we can give the character a minute to get her bearings again. When she's had some time to recover, she's ready for the Thought phase. Here we explore exactly why she's so surprised—because, in our example, this revelation is something that the hero could've told her. It's something she would understand and that would have even made her happy, if he had just told her, and he knew that—but he's chosen to lie to her about it the whole time they've known one another.

That leads us to the Decision. The Decision can be about the coming Action and set up the next scene—or it can be a further decision about the emotional response. In our example, the character begins to grow indignant. You know what? He should have told her. How dare he not? And if he could lie about that, what else about their relationship was a lie?

Now she's mad. We've effectively taken a character from the depths of shock to anger in a few short paragraphs. Using this framework to guide emotional changes in the reaction time between scenes helps to keep the emotional flow rather than giving your readers emotional whiplash from sudden, mercurial changes.

Emotional balance

There's a fine balance to conveying emotion on the page. Too little emotion, and our readers won't feel anything either. Too much, and we risk turning our readers off.

Too little emotion

Emotion is vital to fiction. Without emotion, our books can read like bad history textbooks: a log of who did what, where, and when. Some history stories are moving enough to catch our imagination, but those are rare. If we want our readers to care about our stories—our characters—we have to grab our readers (and our characters) by the emotions.

It's dangerous to run under the assumption that readers will infer how a character feels based purely on the setup. This inevitably leads to that dreaded feedback: "This scene drags. It's boring."

While as the writer, we might have a hard time anyone could be oblivious to our character's emotional plight, if we don't actually show that plight during the scene, for all the readers can see, the character *doesn't* care. She's impassively watching the scene unfold, or participating without any trouble. Setting up a situation just isn't enough: you have to show how that situation affects the character as it unfolds, or the reader will have to assume it's not affecting the character at all.

I learned this lesson well in a scene from a forthcoming novel, *Saints & Spies.* This particular scene fell about halfway through the novel, and the plotline was well established. We'd shown how the character, Molly Malone, felt about the situation, so I believed I didn't have to include her emotional reactions to the scene, in fact, that it was better if I underplayed the emotion. Unfortunately, I underplayed the emotion right out of the scene!

Here's the first version of the scene, where Molly is meeting with LDS missionaries at her friend Lucy's apartment, along with a very persistent suitor, Brian. (In the main plot, Molly is fighting her feelings for the new priest of her parish, Father Tim.)

"Sister Malone." Elder Franklin waited for her to look at him. "We want you to know this for yourself. Will you pray to know the Book of Mormon is the word of God?"

Molly hoped her surprise wasn't apparent. After their extremely obvious hints that she could pray about the Book of Mormon, she didn't expect them to come right out and ask her to.

Elder Franklin pressed on. "I promise as you ask Heavenly Father to know the Book of Mormon is true, He will answer your prayers and, just like Moroni said, you'll come to know the truth of all things through the power of the Holy Ghost. I know the Book of Mormon is true and our Father in Heaven answers prayers."

She nodded. All evening she'd found no way to respond to their entreaties and earnestness. In fact, something about their intent sincerity was what probably touched Molly most. They were young. They were not yet well educated, though they clearly knew their scriptures. Nothing about these young men, or Lucy or especially Brian, should have convinced her of their somewhat outlandish story.

Yet she was about to accept their proposition.

And what would Father Tim think? Could she let that keep her from learning more about the comfort she felt when she read their scriptures? What could it hurt to pray about it?

"Will you, Sister Malone?" Elder Ehrisman echoed his companion's question.

Again, Molly looked at the expectantly hopeful light in the eyes of the quartet surrounding her.

"I will."

Lucy, Brian and the missionaries all broke into instant grins, Brian's the widest of all. He threw an arm around her shoulders and squeezed. Even Brian, who'd initially impressed her as rather indecent, was absolutely sincere when it came to his religion. And that made him tolerable, at least. And, she reminded herself during his prayer, probably a better choice as a romantic interest than a priest.

Suddenly uneasy, Molly had to force herself to smile at each of them as they bid their goodbyes, the elders heading off to another appointment and Brian going to play "church ball." When he mentioned something about Molly coming along to cheer for him, she volunteered to help with the dinner dishes.

In this passage, Molly does show emotions, but they're more intellectualized as she ponders what's happening, rather than visceral reactions to what she's experiencing.

This is where I received the dreaded "It's boring" feedback myself. Although I resisted the change at first, finally I realized ·that my readers weren't seeing Molly's emotions because I'd neglected to put Molly's emotional responses on the page.

This is the version of the scene that was included in the manuscript that was accepted by a publisher:

"Molly." Elder Franklin filled his voice and his wide brown eyes with sincerity. "Will you pray to know the Book of Mormon is the word of God?"

Surprise cleared every thought from her mind. After their extremely obvious hints she could pray about the Book of Mormon, she didn't expect them to come right out and ask.

Elder Franklin pressed on. "He'll answer you, I promise. And I know the Book of Mormon is true."

She nodded, trying to ignore her clammy palms. She was about to accept their proposition. What would Father Tim think? But what could it hurt to pray about it?

> "Will you, Molly?" Elder Ehrisman echoed his companion's question.
>
> Again, Molly looked at the expectantly hopeful light in the eyes of the quartet surrounding her. She tucked her hands under her tweed skirt. "All right."
>
> Lucy, Brian and the missionaries all broke into instant grins, Brian's the widest. He threw an arm around her shoulders and squeezed. Molly waited two long seconds to pull free. She forced a smile as they bid the elders goodbye. Brian stayed to hem and haw about his lame knee and the nursing he needed—until Molly asked him to help clean. He left in under a minute.

Perhaps the most noticeable difference between theses versions is the length and diction. The speech is more natural, and the scene has been pared down considerably. And yet in a much smaller space, we have more emotional responses. Rather than analytically hoping her surprise isn't apparent, readers see her surprise as she experiences it. They see the clammy palms which she tucks under her skirt and her response, an action, to Brian's insistent affections.

Now, not only do we watch what she experiences, but we know what she feels, what's at stake, what's driving her. If the author does it right, the readers feel what she feels. And that's the way to create powerful characters and stories.

Too much emotion

On the other end of the spectrum, we also have to be careful to avoid too much emotion. Overwhelming our readers can turn them off our story or even confuse them. This is especially true in highly emotional scenes. We've all heard the adage, "If the character cries, the reader doesn't have to."

The longer a reader watches a character experience a deep, painful emotion, the more the reader has the chance to analyze, disagree or simply become uncomfortable. We don't want our carefully constructed sympathy to turn to alarm, and we don't want to torture our readers. Too much emotion can pull them out of the story. The emotion may be overwrought or melodramatic, or perhaps it trips your readers' sensitive emotional shutoff valve.

Finding the balance

How can you avoid using too much or too little emotion? We need to know when and how to portray emotion to make sure we don't turn our readers off.

Set it up in advance

Don't drop an emotional scene out of nowhere, without giving the readers some frame of reference. Foreshadow. Set it up. Give them a chance to find out how the character feels about others in the scene or the general situation or similar events. Then it's safe to let the reader feel along with the character with a lot fewer emotion words. But these passages are usually at the end of an emotional setup—that is, the author sets up the emotional situation so that the reader knows what the stakes are, and then there's the moment of emotional release.

Even then, as I learned, there's a fine line between subtle and just plain underdone.

Make it clear in the scene, but don't beat readers over the head

Make sure the emotion is on the page, and show it in a fresh and unique way. Common, overused gestures probably won't convey the full range of your character's nuanced emotions, so work to make it perfectly clear. The readers don't need to be reminded of her love or hatred every five lines, and they don't need paragraphs about the feelings, but do make sure it's actually in there.

Use emotional imagery, setting or props

Going along with the physical sensation of emotions, physical objects in the setting—whether scenery or props—can imbue even more meaning and resonance into a scene. As editor/author Alicia Rasley points out: "We really do endow things with emotional significance (wedding ring!), so that works better for me than emotion WORDS, which are necessarily a step removed."

Especially when we've set up a symbol or given an object additional emotional significance, these props or settings can be so powerful that they can carry most of the emotion in the scene.

Know when to put it in, and when not to

A number of factors influence the use and distribution of emotion in a scene. One of them is pacing: if the scene is fast paced and the emotional beat is short, don't delve too deeply into it. On the other hand, if the scene is slower paced or a major emotional turning point, we'll want to develop those emotions more, showing them to their fullest extent.

Get feedback

Probably the most important step is to get some objective eyes on the scene. When you already know what emotion you want to convey, it's very easy to see it on the page, inferring something the reader wouldn't. Another set of eyes helps to make sure you're finding a good balance and effectively conveying that emotion.

Emotion is tricky to get right, in life and in fiction. However, effective emotion makes our character seem more realistic to our readers. Only cardboard characters lack real emotions or real depth to those emotions. Writing emotion well is worth the effort required to create a well-rounded character.

5

Plot Considerations for Character Depth

Character and plot are intertwined. Character motivations, the antagonist and showing the character's world beyond that of the story help to create deeper characters.

Character and plot, as we've previously seen, are inextricably intertwined. When well executed, plot leads to character—showing us what kind of person we need to create and how to make them realistic—and character leads back to plot through well-motivated choices. So when we're creating realistic characters, we need to take the plot into consideration.

Forcing our character to make difficult choices and impossible decisions through the plot helps to deepen our character. Plotting alone could (and will) fill another volume and more. However, we cannot leave the discussion of character depth without touching on a few of the most important aspects of character depth as shown in the plot.

Difficult choices, deep characters

While a number of plot considerations help to add depth to our characters, forcing our characters to face impossible choices is one of the most effective. We've already worked to establish our character's sympathy with the reader, getting the reader onboard with the character and her goals. Once the reader identifies with the character in this way, if we force the character to face an impossible choice, we draw the reader into the story even more and make the character and her dilemma even more realistic for the reader.

One example of this that struck me recently is in the Victor Hugo novel *Les Misérables*. Jean Valjean shows strengths both physically and in his sense of morality. He struggles with the temptation to steal to survive, and with simply surviving throughout the book, nearly losing his life multiple times. He sacrificed for his family, stealing a loaf of bread to feed his sister's family and spending five years in jail (plus fourteen for escape attempts). Hugo's first task in this wide-ranging novel is establishing reader identification.

Once the reader's on board with Valjean (and other characters introduced in the meantime), Hugo forces him to face an impossible choice. Readers know Valjean is a wanted man, and Inspector Javert is closing in on him. However, at the last minute, Valjean is offered a reprieve: Javert informs him that they've apprehended the "real" Jean Valjean, who's due to be sentenced.

Now, the ever-moral Valjean faces an impossible choice: lie and let this stranger take the punishment for his crimes, or sacrifice the life he's built for himself by telling the truth.

For our character, we can work to pit her motivations and goals against her *other* conflicting motivations and goals. This isn't always easy, but I find that the best character development and the best plots tend to do this. They set up the character wanting two things—say, to get the girl and to capture the bad guy—and then engineer a way to make them mutually exclusive. The girl turns out to the be the bad guy's daughter.

We can even draw out the tension of this choice by increasing what's at stake with each alternative. He's really falling for this girl, and her father threatens anyone who hurts her. Meanwhile, his job is on the line. Then we can make his job even more important by giving him another dependent, perhaps a suddenly ailing parent.

While we don't want to veer into melodrama or stack the consequences so high that it becomes unrealistic, any time we force the character to choose between two things he desperately wants or even needs, the more the reader gets to see the character's thought process, morality and value system—vital components to his realism.

Character motivations

Our character's actions should be what drives most of the plot forward. She makes choices and acts on those goals, and that action causes further complications, driving toward that final climax.

However, to keep a reader relating to the character, these choices and actions must make sense. A well-rounded character does things for reasons that the reader understands, even if the reader doesn't necessarily agree with the actions.

How can we show these motivations, and how can we use them to our advantage as writers, especially when we need the character to do something that might not normally be in line with who he is? We must find what motivates them.

As I put more emphasis on figuring out what motivates my characters, what makes them tick, I not only know how to manipulate them better to still accomplish the purposes of the plot (if not the exact scenes I was planning), but I also know the characters themselves better, making them more well-rounded and realistic.

I used this as part of a combination of techniques to take my manuscript *Saints & Spies* from a quick rejection to an acceptance at the same publisher (although ultimately, we couldn't reach a contractual agreement). For me, my character motivation revelation came at a high level. Originally, I wrote a novel where Molly, the heroine, was somewhat wishy-washy. Halfway through the book, I "discovered" that she was an ex-cop. Trying to integrate those two polar opposite motivations and desires just didn't work. Molly no longer made sense as a character—she was incoherent.

Finally, I let go of the wishy-washy side of her nature. I changed Molly's motivations throughout the book. Instead of being frightened by the villains, she was trying to protect other people from them. Instead of backing down, she stood up and fought. Instead of keeping quiet, she kept dangerous secrets for the sake of others.

This changed a whole lot about her, but the plot actions of the story were largely (though not totally) the same. Molly became a character not to be pitied, but someone you'd want on your side in a fight—and her motivations and her character as a whole finally made sense.

Motivation is important in character choices so that our story continues to feel like the character's actions are driving the plot instead of looking like we authors are manipulating the characters and plot like marionettes. A well-motivated choice sets up the scene, flows well from the previous scene, makes sense to the reader, and most of all, makes the character feel realistic.

Strengthening the villain

Our characters are only as strong as the conflict that they face.

When we force our characters to make difficult choices or to go up against impossible odds, our characters become more real.

Sometimes a key to creating deeper characters is to put more time and effort into the antagonist opposing them. A well-developed antagonist has clear motivations, presents an increasing challenge throughout the story, and always acts at the top of her capability.

Antagonists' motivations

"To be evil" is not a sufficient motivation for the villain's heinous actions in our story. We want our villains to be rounded characters with believable motivations, not just amorphous evil that our hero's got to defeat. They must have a dog in this fight or they'll cash in their chips and go home. So why *this* person? Why *this* (despicable) action? It could be something as simple as money—but there are lots of ways to make money. Why *this* way?

Sometimes, we must revise our antagonist's actions to make our protagonist stronger. Perhaps we need to make our antagonist worse, stronger or a bigger threat. Maybe he needs a bigger goal to pursue. As we put more and more things important to the protagonist in jeopardy, we give the protagonist more reasons and opportunities to react, to see why he needs to grow, and to do that growing.

Brainstorming more depth for our antagonist may help us discover more depth in our protagonist, by giving us more to work with to oppose the protagonist. Working on our antagonist's motivations can help us see our protagonist's motivations more clearly or helping us see how our protagonist must learn and grow. And of course, the more we know about why our antagonist is doing what she's doing, the more potential for conflict we have in our story.

Increasing conflict

James Scott Bell gives excellent advice on better arming the antagonist in *Revision and Self-Editing*, drawing on his "three aspects of death":

- Does the opposition have the power to kill your Lead, like a mafia don, for instance?
- Does the opposition have the power to crush your Lead's professional pursuits, like a crooked judge in a criminal trial?
- Does the opposition have the power to crush your Lead's spirit? Think of the awful mother played by Gladys Cooper in the 1942 film *Now, Voyager*. She has that power over her daughter, played by Bette Davis. (229)

Bell's advice is useful across genres because it applies to more than just life-and-death suspense. Make sure as you arm your opposition that they don't become "a caricature," Bell warns—show their shades of gray, their dimensions and emotions. And if you end up making your opposition stronger than your Lead, strengthen your Lead to match the villain next.

Maximum capacity

An antagonist must always act at the top of her capability to present a true challenge for our character. If our antagonist makes a stupid choice, acting at less than her maximum capacity, in order for our character to win the day, it cheapens our character's victory. Sure, he wins when she makes a dumb mistake, but would he be so lucky if she weren't having an off day? We want our protagonist to triumph not because of luck but because he's strong enough to beat the antagonist even when the antagonist is as powerful as she's ever been.

Climactic conflict

Our well-rounded character will ultimately show her strength in the climax where she confronts the villain. At this point, our character is finally stronger than the antagonist—usually because of the journey of inner growth the external events of the story has put her through. This final showdown is our greatest opportunity to not only show the strength of our villain, but the new strength of our main character, especially as she uses what she's learned to defeat the antagonist and become a better person.

Any narrative must work toward this climax. Weak, episodic fiction jumps from one event to another without building toward that final moment. Instead, we want to gradually but inevitably build toward that moment when the protagonist must finally face her inner fears and demons and make the change for the better, defeating external antagonists along the way.

If our character is defined by the villain she defeats, we need to make sure that the peak of the dramatic journey for her coincides with the internal journey's peak and comes at nearly the end of the story. The more difficult we make this final decision for the characters, the more satisfying a believable conclusion will be.

For more discussion on using arcs at the climax, see *Character Arcs*.

A life outside the story

We want our readers to feel as though our character will live on once they close the book. To do that, we must give the reader a sense that the character wasn't born on page one (unless, of course, they were), and that they have a history and a life that will continue beyond the end of the story.

Aspirations

An important part of the character's life outside the story, especially at the outset, is showing that the character has goals and aspirations beyond the context of the story. Some of these goals may be met by the end of the story; some of them may not. Simply having a lifelong dream helps to make a character feel more real.

A careful balance is necessary here. We don't want to leave readers feeling unfulfilled if our character won't end up any closer to these major life goals. However, if our character's emotional journey leads him to be more ready to tackle that lifelong dream, it can tie into a beautiful and fulfilling ending.

For example, let's say our character has a lifelong dream of earning his pilot's license. However, his fear of heights is holding him back. When we dig deeper into this character's fear of heights in our prewriting process, we can see that it's a manifestation of his fear of uncertainty.

Early on in our story, we may use his goal to get a pilot's license and the fear that's holding him back to illustrate the untenable position he's in emotionally. Through the external events of the plot—which may very well have nothing to do with flying a plane—we'll send the character on a journey of growth to overcome his fear of uncertainty.

At the climax of the story, we'll show him conquering this fear at a critical moment despite his uncertainty. Then, in the last little scene of resolution, we'll show our character signing up for flying lessons. Although the pilot's license aspiration isn't fulfilled within the confines of the story, readers see the character has not only learned his lesson of emotional growth but he's living on to live out his dreams.

Simple subplots like these tend to add a lot of depth to our characters, making them very realistic. But that doesn't mean we should throw every possible detail and passing whim into our stories.

What to take out

Naturally, not everything we know about our characters will make it into our story. Judicious editing—including self-editing—is crucial to creating the illusion of a character and a story that makes sense. Readers need a sense that the character has goals and a past outside the story, but they don't need to see all of that described in minute detail.

So how can we tell what to include? As we've mentioned before, my two major guidelines for whether something is worthy to be included in a story are:

- Does this advance the plot?

- Does this show the reader something vital about the character and/or her emotional journey in the context of the story?

We might be intimately familiar with the character's past relationships, but we don't need his dating curriculum vitae presented on page one—or anywhere else in the story, necessarily. If we mention his failed relationship with that really needy widow, our readers will assume it's significant. They'll be on the lookout for how that relates to the external plot of the present story or to the character and his journey. If it doesn't, instead of making the character seem more "real," it just feels like a distraction that detracts from the story.

If our story is about a woman who is dealing with control issues, it may be significant that she recently lost a hundred pounds. That detail is hinting at or even revealing a deeper issue about the character. On the other hand, if our story is about her repairing her relationship with her father (who never cared one way or the other about her weight), mentioning that detail is superfluous. Minutiae doesn't enhance our characters or give the illusion of depth.

To tie into our example from the aspirations section, let's return to our character who has always dreamed of earning his pilot's license but has let his fear of heights hold him back. Let's reimagine his story, that instead of facing his fear of uncertainty (and heights), he's coming to grips with his wife's death. His wife had nothing to do with his fear of heights or his goal to fly, and his emotional journey of grief and healing doesn't relate back to that fear.

Cramming a mention of his pipe dream doesn't make him feel more realistic. It may make him seem flighty and distractible, and it distracts our readers as they try to decipher the significance of his goal, when really, it isn't significance in the context of this plot and emotional journey. Readers can tell when we include something just for the sake of generating artificial character depth. Instead, strive for true depth and make the character truly come to life.

Realistic and well-executed motivations, a challenging antagonist and a life outside the story all help to put the finishing touches on our deep character. When we use these techniques in tandem with our previous ones, our realistic, coherent, distinctive character practically leaps off the page.

CHARACTER DEPTH EXAMPLES

No study of character would be complete
without examples of its execution:
well-rounded, realistic characters
that live on with readers.

We all have favorite characters who seem to live on in our imaginations long after we close the book they're featured in. These characters are often great examples of characters who show real depth. Here are just a few examples, including suggestions from fellow readers and writers.

HARRY POTTER

J. K. Rowling's universe of Harry Potter is so real to readers that it has blossomed into a movie franchise, a popular theme park and more. Characters are one important reason why this series has been so well received.

Harry Potter himself

Harry himself is, naturally, the most popular character at the center of his universe. As the main character, naturally, he's shown with great detail. His appearance strongly influences how other people see him—especially people who knew his parents. He's small for his age, and his aunt and uncle take advantage of him terribly. These physio- and sociological dimensions combine to create a Harry who is lonely and unsure of himself.

Rowling devotes much of the opening of the series to developing sympathy with him, almost to the point of making him a sad sack. We get to see his backstory in the opening chapter—orphaned, his parents murdered by Voldemort, Harry's left on his aunt's doorstep. The subsequent chapters show how badly Harry is mistreated in his aunt's home. Rowling works hard to get readers on board the emotional roller coaster here.

Rowling made a stylistic choice to not a POV that is not always very deep, especially in the cinematic opening chapter which gives us a "wide-angle lens" view of the world Harry will grow up in. (As an infant, Harry isn't in much of a position to give us a glimpse into his world.) We remain focused pretty tightly on Harry and his goals and dreams, however. Rowling uses devices such as the Mirror of Erised ("desire" spelled backward) to reveal Harry's desires, increasing his sympathy and propelling the plot.

Rowling also frequently engineers the plot and circumstances to work against Harry. As a child, he's frequently powerless to change his situation, such as when someone in power is unkind to him (Professor Snape, Dolores Umbridge). These struggles go beyond his sad-sack backstory, but Harry shows his strength by persevering. More importantly, in his ultimate conflict, Harry is also facing off against the most dangerous, fearsome wizard in generations. His choices aren't easy and he's tempted to take the easy route. However, his sense of morality ultimately prevails and he saves the day.

Ron Weasley

Ron quickly becomes Harry's best friend. He helps to show Harry's depth as a character by not only giving him a relationship to help indirectly characterize them both, but to contrast Harry's own life. Where Harry is unloved and neglected, he's also wealthy, talented at school and Quidditch, and famous. Ron isn't any of these things: loved, but harried, poor, middling at school and Quidditch, known only by his family's reputation. His character helps to humanize and humble Harry.

Ron also shows character depth himself in how fully imagined his relationships are. He has five older brothers and a younger sister, all of whom have lives. His parents, although not at Hogwarts, are very involved in his life, and are depicted well themselves. Ron cares about his siblings, is jealous of them, jokes with them.

Not all his relationships are so positive. Part of Ron's function in the story is to explain the wizarding world to newcomer Harry, including the social tensions between "classes" of wizards. Draco Malfoy makes his entrance sneering at Ron, and his father's job and the family's poverty. Ron knows Draco's family as well. Even though they're only children, Ron and Draco have interactions and a relationship that reflect the world they live in—and help to bring them and that world to life for the reader.

Hermione Granger

Although Hermione is a secondary character whose POV we do not use in the story, she too lives on in readers' imaginations. She earns reader sympathy by having her own goals while also helping Ron and Harry. Because she's self-motivated, the reader has the opportunity to get on board with her journey. She doesn't simply exist to further the plot or act as a foil for Harry and his adventures. Hermione is a willing participant in those adventures.

At the same time, however, Hermione doesn't just do things for Harry because he's got a charming smile or because she's only in the story to play into Harry's plot line. To the contrary—Hermione presses forward in her agenda and never swoons over her famous friend. Hermione has her plans set out and lives according to them, even when they don't quite fit within the confines of the story.

Harry, Ron and Hermione come to life for readers, as do many other characters in the books.

SCOUT, *TO KILL A MOCKINGBIRD*

Harper Lee created a character that has truly come to life for millions of readers. Although Scout is only a child in the story present here, she's able to convey her story through powerful words. The POV in *To Kill a Mockingbird* is quite deep, showing us more of Scout's own thoughts and weaving her voice through the emotions of a confusing event in childhood.

Here, the plot also has a great influence on character depth. Scout and especially her father Atticus face some difficult choices about morality. Because they stand up for the right in the face of danger and the antagonists who have the power to hurt them physically, Atticus and his children are placed in jeopardy. The antagonist in the story could well claim Scout's life—and nearly does. It's Scout's bravery, and her innocent insistence upon doing the right thing, that remain with readers for years.

ELIZABETH BENNET, *PRIDE AND PREJUDICE*

Elizabeth Bennet has become one of the most enduring characters in English literature. Jane Austen carefully crafted her main character's sympathy. Obviously, deep POV was not yet in vogue when Austen was writing. Instead, Austen employed an omniscient narrator, often commenting on society or from society's perspective, as well as a third-person limited mode conveying Elizabeth's viewpoint. Yet readers are still able to connect deeply with Elizabeth's thoughts and feelings—the most important goal of deep POV and a key part of conveying a well-rounded character.

Austen works hard to create character sympathy for Elizabeth. She's offstage in the first chapter and only has three lines of dialogue in the second chapter, so readers' first real encounter with her character is through her parents discussing her in the first chapter. In this direct characterization, we're told she isn't as pretty or as good humored as her sisters, but her father favors her because of her "quickness." This wit, which we see throughout the book, is her chief strength.

Elizabeth's first real scene comes in chapter. Mr. Bingley has brought his friend, Mr. Darcy, to his estate and to a ball. At first, Darcy makes quite a stir, being rich, noble and handsome, but when the crowd sees how conceited he is, the tide of their favor turns against him, especially once he rejects Elizabeth as a dance partner. But he doesn't just turn her down; he claims his reason is that another man has slighted her, heaping another insult upon her.

She won't allow herself to be crushed by the judgment of a man nobody likes anyway, of course. But this embarrassment at being slighted is the beginning of her struggles. More subtly, her struggles are woven throughout as we also get to see others' harsh judgments of her and her family. This use of dramatic irony can be an advantage of omniscient POV.

Elizabeth shows the last characteristic of character sympathy, sacrifice, when her older sister takes ill while going for a short visit to the Bingleys and must stay there to convalesce. When word reaches them the next day, Elizabeth is concerned enough for her sister to walk the three miles to the Bingleys' and stay there to care for her. The walk, she insists, is nothing, but the exertion puts her into a bit of disarray, especially to be seen by society people who are already conceited about how much better they are than these "country folk." But her sister's welfare is more important to Elizabeth than anyone's opinion.

Throughout the next few chapters, we see two defining features of Elizabeth: her wit and her prejudice. She's quick to judge not only Darcy by Mr. Bingley and his sisters quite harshly. (While she's off-scene, it does seem that this judgment, at least of the women, is justified). The prejudice sets up her character weakness.

Mr. Darcy's pride and Elizabeth Bennet's prejudice against him interfere in their relationship. Slowly, Mr. Darcy reveals his true nature, and humbles himself as he helps Elizabeth's sisters despite their low station and sometimes inappropriate behavior. Elizabeth juggles her often-inappropriate mother and her own tendencies to let her wit run wild, and is embarrassed by Mr. Darcy even more, until she ultimately must sacrifice her own pride and admit her prejudice—and that she was wrong in her judgment. She learns she was too quick to judge Mr. Darcy, and although she prided herself on her wisdom, she needs to re-evaluate the evidence and her previous estimation of Mr. Darcy.

FURTHER EXAMPLES

Many friends generously supplied several more examples of their favorite well-depicted characters. I couldn't fit in an analysis of all of their choices, but they deserve further study.

Books and authors

- *The Scorpio Races* by Maggie Stiefvater: "It is in deep POV and it is just beautiful." – Carol Storey-Costley
- The Farseer Trilogy, The Liveship Traders trilogy, The Tawny Man trilogy and The Rain Wilds Chronicle by Robin Hobb: "She does characters well. She does everything well. She is the only author that I cried when the bad guy died." – Carol Storey-Costley
- Nancy Drew series, Caroline Keene
- *The House Next Door* by Anne Rivers Siddons: "The protagonist believes that an architect is evil and causing deaths to happen in the houses he designs. Tragedies befall the people who live in them. She believes that his houses are killing people and that he is the enemy. An interesting twist is that she turns out to be the killer in that she ends up killing the architect. In this case, her emotional turmoil escalates and it ties into the conflict of the story by her becoming the actual killer (the evil)." – Janet Kerr
- Mark Twain

- J. R. R. Tolkien
- Ally Carter
- Lloyd Alexander
- Carol O'Connell

Characters

- Haley Mills in *Pollyanna*, when she finally tells her aunt what she really thinks of her
- Gandalf, *The Lord of the Rings* by J. R. R. Tolkien
- Josh Hobbs, *Bone by Bone* by Carol O'Connell: "Josh Hobbs is actually dead throughout the book. He is only described by another character, but his personality, his talent, all the little details about him, his favorite color, his belonging, all of it raises my hope for him to be alive some way—or worse, I really hope that he is the bad guy behind all the chaos. Anything is better than him being dead." – Syakira Sungkar
- Anthony Lockwood, Lockwood & Co. Series by Jonathan Groud
- Bartimaeus, Bartimaeus Series by Jonathan Groud
- Mr. Norrell, *Jonathan Strange & Mr. Norrell* by Susanna Clarke
- Dutchy, *Orphan Train* by Christina Baker Kline
- A, Pretty Little Liars Series by Sara Shepard
- Peeta Mellark, The Hunger Games Series by Suzanne Collins
- Clarice Starling, *Silence of the Lambs* by Thomas Harris: "Clarice's emotional turmoil is evident in her wound as a child. When the lambs went to slaughter and they started screaming she tried to save one by picking it up

and running with it. She still hears their screaming when she is under stress. This ties into the conflict in the story in that as an adult, (interesting that the story opens with her running and the book is named after her wound) her job is trying to save a victim of a serial killer. Much of the show/book is the kidnapped victim screaming. Clarice goes through a continual emotional upheaval with Lecter as she tries to pry information out of him to find the victim. He gets in her head and in ours (the reader) and makes her relive the anguish that ties in well with the story." – Janet Kerr

- Menolly, Harper Hall trilogy by Anne McCaffrey: "I love female characters with their own agendas." – Michelle Goddard
- Eddie Dean, The Dark Tower series by Stephen King: "We meet Eddie when he is a lowlife junkie, and through the course of the series, watch him grow into the heart of a ragtag group of people putting their lives on the line to save the world from ancient forces of evil. What I love most about Eddie is his complete and believable transformation." – Jean-Paul Bass
- Sue Trinder, *Fingersmith* by Sarah Waters. "Sue is in way over her head but she doesn't know it, and neither does the reader. I had a lot of sympathy for her, even as she works to have someone locked away for money, and when the tables are turned, I was just as shocked as Sue because I was so in her head, I didn't even think to question what she was telling me." – Jean-Paul Bass
- Eugenides and both queens, *The Queen of Attolia* by Megan Whalen Turner: "Eugenides is my all-time favorite character, though. He possesses a great balance between 'genius' and 'flawed.'" – Heather Baird

- Sage, *The False Prince* by Jennifer A. Nielsen
- Shevraeth *et. al., Crown Duel/Court Duel* by Sherwood Smith

CONCLUDING ON CHARACTER DEPTH

Character depth is a complex and multi-faceted concept. No single technique alone can make your character seem like a real person, and all of the vital, interrelated methods of creating character depth require thought in planning, care in execution and refining in revisions. It's not easy.

But writing characters and fiction that are well-developed is never easy. We can't expect to get everything right on the first draft. Revision and feedback are vital to getting our characters right as well.

As we key into the techniques that help to create and convey realistic characters, we can become more successful at creating these integrated, coherent people. We can build characters who truly come to life for our readers, keeping our readers engaged in their stories and pondering that character long after they finish the book. Well-developed characters with real depth make our stories compelling and leave our readers satisfied—and clamoring for more.

REFERENCES

WORKS CITED

Aristotle. *Poetics.*

Bell, James Scott. *Write Great Fiction: Revision and Self-Editing.* Cincinnati, OH: Writer's Digest, 2008.

Bickham, Jack M. *Scene and Structure.* Cincinnati, OH: Writer's Digest, 1993.

Egri, Lajos. *The Art of Dramatic Writing: Its Basis in the Creative Interpretation of Human Motives.* New York: Simon and Schuster, 1960.

Hauge, Michael in Gold, Jami. "Michael Hauge's Workshop: Combining Emotional Journeys and External Plots." Jami Gold, Paranormal Author. <http://jamigold.com/2012/08/michael-hauges-workshop-making-emotional-journeys-and-external-plots-play-together/>.

Lawson, Margie. Empowering Character Emotions Course. Lecture packets and live courses available through MargieLawson.com.

Mystery Man on Film (Pseudonymous). "The 'Raiders'

Story Conference." Mystery Man on Film. <http://mysterymanonfilm.blogspot.com/2009/03/r aiders-story-conference.html>.

Rasley, Alicia. Comment on "Emotion—Less is More?" Edittorrent. <http://edittorrent.blogspot.com/2008/09/ emotion-less-is-more.html?showComment= 1220584200000#c456407678213314296>.

Rhamey, Ray. "Free FtQ chapter—showing and telling." Flogging the Quill. <http://www.floggingthequill.com/flogging_the_q uill/2011/02/free-ftq-chaptershowing-and-telling.html>.

Snyder, Blake. *Save the Cat!: The Last Book on Screenwriting You'll Ever Need.* Studio City, CA: M. Wiese Productions, 2005.

EXAMPLES CITED

Austen, Jane. *Pride and Prejudice.*

Frozen. Dir. Christopher Buck and Jennifer Lee. Perf. Idina Menzel and Kristen Bell. Walt Disney Pictures, 2013.

Hugo, Victor. *Les Misérables.*

Indiana Jones and the Raiders of the Lost Ark. Dir. Stephen Spielberg. Perf. Harrison Ford and Karen Allen. Paramount, 1981.

Lee, Harper. *To Kill a Mockingbird.* New York: HarperCollins: 1960.

McCollum, Jordan. *Saints & Spies.* Pleasant Grove, Utah: Durham Crest, forthcoming.

O'Neill, Craig. "End Run." *Burn Notice.* USA. 18 June 2009. Television.

Rowling, J. K. *Harry Potter and the Sorcerer's Stone.* New York: Scholastic, 1998.

Shrek. Dir. Andrew Adamson and Vicky Jenson. Perf. Mike Myers, Eddie Murphy and Cameron Diaz. Dreamworks, 2011.

You may also refer to reader-submitted list of examples at the end of chapter six.

FURTHER READING

A few selected resources I think are especially helpful in understanding character depth.

Campbell, Joseph. *The Hero with a Thousand Faces.* Princeton, NJ: Princeton UP, 1968.

Collins, Brandilyn. *Getting into Character: Seven Secrets a Novelist Can Learn from Actors.* New York: John Wiley & Sons, Inc., 2002.

Frey, James N. *How to Write a Damn Good Novel.* New York: St. Martin's, 1987.

Hardy, Janice. "Why Character Arcs (and Growth) Make Readers Care." *The Other Side of the Story.* 25 Feb. 2013. <http://blog.janicehardy.com/2013/02/why-character-arcs-and-growth-make.html>.

McCollum, Jordan. *Character Arcs: Founding, forming and finishing your character's internal journey.* Pleasant Grove, Utah: Durham Crest, 2013.

McCollum, Jordan. *Character Sympathy: Creating characters your readers have to root for.* Pleasant Grove, Utah: Durham Crest, 2014.

INDEX

THANK YOU FOR READING!

If you enjoyed this book,
please tell your writing friends & review it online.

To sign up for information on upcoming releases, please visit
http://JordanMcCollum.com/newsletter/

Find character depth worksheets and examples at my website:
http://JordanMcCollum.com/character-depth/

Writing Craft Classes!

I'm now offering classes on writing craft through my website! Topics include character depth, character arcs, structural self-editing and more!

Class sizes are kept small to feature personal interaction and hands-on help. Lesson materials go beyond an overview of the topics presented to dig into how to apply those techniques in your current work.

Be sure to join my mailing list to be the first to hear about future class schedules and topics!

http://JordanMcCollum.com/newsletter/

Writing Craft Series

Character Sympathy

Out now

Whether your character is an angel or a devil, your readers
need to be onboard to want to read on. Create character
sympathy to draw your readers in and get them rooting for
your character.

Tension, Conflict & Suspense

Coming soon

What keeps a reader glued to your novel no matter what the
hour? Tension and suspense. Blend these techniques with
surprise to keep your readers turning those pages in any genre.

ACKNOWLEDGMENTS

Once again, I have to admit that this book is only possible through the extensive help of others.

As always, my family was an amazing support during the production of this book. Yet again, my husband Ryan did the dishes, listened to me rant about how overburdened I was, and finally held the baby and kept the kids at bay to keep me sane and help me get this book completed. My adorable children, Hayden, Rebecca, Rachel, Hazel and Benjamin, were very patient with their mom, even when she was too stressed to do them the same courtesy. My parents, Ben and Diana Franklin, and my sisters, Jaime, Brooke and Jasmine, have been a support to me throughout my life. My wonderful critique partners, Julie Coulter Bellon and Emily Gray Clawson, provided encouragement and cheering on whenever I needed.

I'm grateful to everyone who participated in my online class "Deepen Your Characters, Deepen Your Fiction," in January and February 2015. The positive responses to the class inspired me to expand my thoughts into a book. Thank you especially to those who helped to refine that information outside of the class: my husband Ryan, my sister Jaime, and my good friends Emily Clawson and Sarah Anderson. And extra special thanks to for being my go-to Harry Potter expert. Also, talented author Susan Dayley deserves special thanks for providing me with an endorsement for this book based on the class material on very short notice.

I also want to thank my wonderful newsletter subscribers who shared with me their favorite characters and authors. Carol Storey-Costley, David M. Goodman, Sr., Andrea Kunz, Syakira Sungkar, Janet Kerr, Michelle Goddard, Jean-Paul Bass, and Heather Baird each provided me with great examples of characters. I wish I could have included an analysis of all of their great examples, but all of their favorite characters are listed in chapter six now. Syakira Sungkar also deserves special thanks for her quick and generous feedback on the advance edition of this book.

As always, I'm grateful to the wonderful authors and bloggers who have helped me learn more about the craft of writing, giving me the tools to process the nuances of storytelling so I could eventually share some of that knowledge. Special credit must go to Larry Brooks, Jami Gold, Janice Hardy, and Alicia Rasley and Theresa Stevens, all of whom selflessly share their expertise on their blogs and websites, and who have been extremely kind to me personally.

ABOUT THE AUTHOR

PHOTO BY JAREN WILKEY

An award-winning fiction author, Jordan McCollum enjoys teaching through her writing craft blog at JordanMcCollum.com, through live and online classes, and in her Writing Craft series. For three years, she served as the inaugural Education Director of Authors Incognito, an online writers' support group with over four hundred members. On the fiction side, she is the author of four Whitney Award–finalist novels in the romantic suspense series Spy Another Day. She makes her home in Utah with her husband and their five children.

Made in the USA
San Bernardino, CA
08 October 2015